"There are three types o
for: Moms that love being

needs, and entrepreneurs that are able to build a successful business. Any one of those alone is a daunting task.

Then you have Janette Gleason, who apparently didn't get the memo that those were hard. Janette took being a mom, raised a child with special needs, added a successful business, and somehow still finds time to give back and help those around her.

It is my personal belief that we are on this earth to achieve greatness. Janette is doing that. If you have a chance to work with, meet, or get to know her, take it. I guarantee it will be worth your time."

~ Brad Martineau, Sixth Division

"Janette is the perfect example of what can happen when someone has a desire to learn and the ability to act. In a very short amount of time she has mastered the art of marketing and process automation. Her story is truly inspiring."

~ Jordan Hatch, Infusionsoft Guru and Ninja Master

"Her unwavering commitment to mapping out our needs in Infusionsoft and her great eye for detail, has meant that Janette has really understood our business needs. I have been amazed a number of times during this process at how well she has translated my requests into really smart Infusionsoft sequences and actions."

~ Lisa Armstrong, Cleancorp

"She not only exceeded our expectations, but has shown us new ways to use Infusionsoft that our programmers had not conceived. You cannot ask for anything more than 'success' from a Success Coach. Working with Janette has been a true pleasure."

~ Rod Neal, USClassics

"I believe the reason Janette is so great with and for her clients is that she's not a "techy". She learned Infusionsoft by implementing it for her and her husband's business, so she learned it from a user's perspective, not a technical perspective. Janette relates so well to business owners because she IS a business owner herself first."

~ Jeff Jones, Interior Expressions Design Showroom

"When I have Janette on my team, I have more confidence that we can complete the campaign with the right strategy. Janette's passion for the "Perfect Customer Lifecycle" helps to create a road map for each campaign. I truly appreciate Janette's calm, methodical approach to working on my marketing projects."

~ Shawn Sandoval, Cooper McManus

"I have been following Janette Gleason's work since she was an Ultimate Marketer finalist on the main stage at InfusionCon in 2011. Janette's story has always resonated with me because I too was a stay at home mom and small business owner. Janette's candidness in this book is a direct reflection of Janette in real life - she speaks from the heart and gives 110% to everything that she does. Janette's story is the hero's journey at its best."

~ Jessica Maes, Maes Consulting

"Janette was like most moms. Wanting what was best for her children and trying to figure out how to make that happen. When suddenly confronted with the idea that one of her children may be dealing with a lifelong and serious disorder her life was turned upside down. Janette faced this challenge head on with determination, grace, and love. I am blessed to have known Janette and her lovely family and want to thank her for putting a real face on the day to day life of receiving a diagnosis of, and living with, Autism."

~ Christy Woosley

"The mother of my children, my wife, my business partner, and my best friend – Janette is everything to me. I am so blessed to have her in my life. I don't know how she does it, but she does. Janette is an inspiration to our children, a passionate entrepreneur, and a great wife. I could not be prouder of everything she has accomplished. She is an amazing Mompreneur."

~ Joe Gleason, Gleason Financial Group, LLC

Confessions of a MOMpreneur

My Journey from Stressed-Out, Stay-at-Home Mom to Successful Entrepreneur

by Janette Gleason

Confessions of a MOMpreneur

My Journey from Stessed-Out, Stay-at-Home Mom to Successful Entrepreneur

www.JanetteGleason.com

© Copyright 2013 by Janette Gleason

Cover design and layout by Hollister Design Group

Published by Gleason Consulting Group, LLC

ISBN # 978-1-4675-6349-9

Dedication

This book is dedicated to love of my life –
my husband, best friend, and business partner,
Joe Gleason. Your love, support, loyalty, and
unwavering ambition give me the strength
to accomplish more than I would have ever
imagined. Thank you for believing in me and for
supporting my dreams. I love you!

I dedicate this book to my children:

To Joey, you are the light of my life. As I tell you
before you go to sleep at night, "You make me
happy. I am so glad God gave me you." You have
made me a better person, and I am so grateful for
the light you shine on me each day.

My dear Jianna, our gracious gift from God, your
smile and giving spirit warm my heart every day.
Your creativity and grace amaze me, and I'm so
proud you are my daughter.

To our sweet Jillian, you are an angel sent from
above. I adore your kindness and gentleness.
Because of your laughter and charm,
my life is filled with joy.

* Table of Contents *

✳ Acknowledgements ✳

To my loving husband, **Joe Gleason** – Thank you for allowing me to pursue my dreams. You have so graciously encouraged me to be "me" and I am so very grateful.

To my children, **Joey, Jianna, and Jillian Gleason** – Thank you for the joy you bring to my life.

To my **Dad** – Thank you for providing a stable and loving home for me and for your continuous support and wisdom throughout the years.

To my **Mom** – Thank you for setting a high standard for me as a mother. I am so grateful for the beautiful home life and safe haven you created for me as a child. Thank you for being my friend, as well as my mother.

To **Mimi and Bill Landwer** – Thank you for allowing me to create your database so many years ago! I remember (going back to the early 90's) when "Mr. Bill" asked me to print labels for a mailing. He handed me the WordPerfect manual, and said, "Here you go! Figure it out." After many hours and hundreds of wasted labels, I did in fact figure it out. I created that database for your small business, and so began my love for database marketing!

To **Ed and Shannon Downey** – Thank you for taking a chance on us and allowing Joe to study your business model. We are also grateful for your "gentle" nudge, which gave us the courage to start our own office in Arizona.

To my friend **Christy Woosley** – Thank you for sharing your time and experience to teach me about autism and for guiding me to find help for Joey. Thank you also for being a strong woman and a role model to me. You gave me strength to fight for Joey, and I am forever grateful.

To Joey's Kindergarten teacher **Lisa Raby** – Thank you for your patience and understanding. Thank you for taking Joey under your wing and taking care of him for so many years. You are angel sent from God to bring peace to our family.

To my friend and Joey's care provider **Jennifer Rasmussen** (Miss Jennifer) – Thank you for your prayers, patience, and unwavering faith and love for Joey and our family. Your impact on all of us is eternal.

To the **Melmed Center** – Thank you for your knowledge about autism spectrum disorders and for giving hope to parents of autistic children. You gave our family clarity and direction when we were confused and feeling helpless.

To our friend **Steve Heideman** – Thank you for introducing us to Infusionsoft! I am also grateful for the many the hours you spent teaching me about sales funnels and drip sequences. It finally sank in, as I told you it would! Thank you also for being an example of strength, courage and faith. We love you!

To **Infusionsoft** – Thank you for creating the ultimate software for small business owners and for supporting the dreams of entrepreneurs around the world.

To Infusionsoft guru **Jordan Hatch** – Thank you for your amazing Mastermind Webinars and for teaching me your elaborate ninja tricks. Thank you for believing in me and giving me the confidence to do some amazing things for our businesses!

To Infusionsoft's Event Coordinator **Nicole Shoots** – Thank you for encouraging me even when I thought I was going to fall apart!

To **Kathy Sacks** – Thank you for believing in me and for your support and guidance. I look to you as an example of success not only in business, but also as a mother.

To **Pamela Slim** – Thank you for teaching me the value of building a community and for being an example of success as an entrepreneur and as a mother. You rank as a respected mentor on my High Council of Jedi Knights!

To **Chuck Trautman** – Thank you for your encouragement and for holding me accountable while writing this book! You have helped me grow as an entrepreneur, and I thank you for your leadership!

To **Sonia Choquette** - Thank you for your wisdom and guidance. You challenge me to work through life's lessons so I may create and live my heart's desire.

To my **clients** – Thank you for allowing me to share in your passion as a small business owner.

✦ Introduction ✦

As I was doing some online research to find out about other mothers who were also entrepreneurs, delightedly I came across the term "Mompreneur." Appropriately, it caught my attention, and I thought to myself, "Yes! There's a name for me!"

Here are a few definitions of Mompreneur that I encountered will surfing the net:

> Mompreneur – New name created to describe a multi-tasking mother who can balance both the stresses of running a home-based business as an entrepreneur, and the time-consuming duties of motherhood at the same time.
>
> ~ www.BusinessDictionary.com

> Mompreneur – A slang term describing women who run their own businesses while also acting as a full time parent. Mompreneurs are more likely to run a business out of the home than out of a commercial building. Because of family obligations, mompreneurs have to balance the requirements of running a business with the demands of their children, and may do the bulk of their work during the time when their children do not require as much attention.
>
> ~ www.Investopedia.com

And my favorite:

> Mompreneur – These are women who bring home the bacon and fry it up in a pan and **finally** get paid for it **without** leaving their homes.
>
> ~ Vickie Jimenez, www.successsystemsnow.com

I am a Mompreneur, and I feel extremely fortunate to be able to pursue my dreams as a business owner yet still able to stay at home to raise our children. Between my international conference calls or coaching sessions, you'll find me doing laundry and prepping for dinner. Between helping out with homework or playing games with my family, you'll find me configuring software and running payroll!

I would never have guessed in a million years that this former elementary school teacher would help own and operate four businesses, teach others how to create marketing campaigns, and help business owners worldwide. God certainly had wonderful plans for me – I just needed to open my eyes to see this new path for my life.

Writing this book and sharing my story took me completely out of my comfort zone, but it has been an incredible journey. I had to revisit some of the darkest hours of my life, and so many terrible feelings and memories resurfaced as I told those stories. I also shed tears of joy while recounting those "turning point" experiences that have brought me to where I am today.

I have tremendous feelings of gratitude for so many people who helped me along the way, and this book tells my journey.

* Part One *

THE BACK STORY

Father Knows Best

As a young girl raised in the Chicago suburbs, I had an extremely traditional upbringing. It was almost like living a *Father Knows Best* episode. My father was a hard-working electrician who made his way from an apprentice to becoming an executive vice president of the company. My mother was a housewife and stayed home to raise my brother, John, and me. While my dad was the sole provider for our family, my mother took care of home matters happily and successfully.

Everything I needed or wanted was provided to me, and I experienced an enriched childhood. From dance lessons, to music lessons, to yearly vacations with my family, I enjoyed my upbringing in a stable and loving home.

I lived in a beautiful home with my family on a quiet

Janette with her father (John), mother (June), and brother (John Jr.) in 1975.

3

neighborhood cul-de-sac. Growing up, my mother doted on me, and I rarely had to lift a finger to do any sort of chore. My mother was a talented

Janette's childhood home in Schaumburg, Illinois.

seamstress and made the most beautiful dresses, cuddly stuffed animals, and darling dolls (all with extensive wardrobes) for me. Our home was always immaculate and orderly, and my mother prepared a delicious, home-cooked meal for our family every night. I give my mother so much credit for doing all that she did for us with such grace and happiness.

I was an especially conscientious child, particularly in school. I loved learning, and I always wanted to get good grades and please my parents. By the time I was in second grade, I had decided I wanted to become an elementary school teacher. I remember quite vividly the day my second grade class was taken to an empty classroom for testing. As I sat there with my number 2 pencil, waiting for my answer sheet (you know, the one with the bubbles), I looked around at the bare walls and bulletin boards. I started imagining what MY classroom would look like. Within minutes, I had that entire room planned out in my mind! I figured out how I would arrange the students' desks and had ideas for each bulletin board in the room. I saw myself standing up by the chalkboard teaching my classroom of students.

I would buy used textbooks at garage sales and play school with my friends and cousins. As you can imagine, when I got my hands on a teacher's manual, I felt as if I had gone to heaven. I, of course, was the teacher and typed out tests on my mom's typewriter and created projects for my "students" well in advance for my upcoming play dates! I just knew that teaching was my passion, and could not get there fast enough!

When I was around ten years old, I began looking after the neighborhood children to give their mothers a break or to allow them to cook and clean in peace. After a couple of years, I had steady babysitting gigs and loved caring for the neighborhood kids. In high school, I started taking child psychology classes and continued finding ways to teach and nurture little ones. I was fortunate enough my senior year to be accepted into a college preparatory program. Because of this program, I was able to go to a nearby elementary school every day to assist the second grade teachers and gain some actual teaching experience.

After graduating high school in 1991, I attended Augustana College (a small liberal arts college in Rock Island, Illinois) with the goal of becoming a teacher. I double-majored in Elementary Education and Spanish and graduated Magna Cum Laude in 1995.

My enthusiastic job search began after graduation. It was a tough market, and I called every school district in a 100-mile radius of the Chicago suburbs. As I worked through the list asking for open positions and sending out my resume, I was getting worried that my dream of becoming a teacher was not going to come true quite yet. I did not give up though, and luckily my persistence paid off.

I called the district of West Chicago (my list was alphabetical, so I was nearing the end) and asked if they were hiring any teachers. The woman on the line asked me if I spoke Spanish. I replied, "Yes, I do!" With excitement in her voice, she asked me if I could come in the next day for an interview. Long story short, I was offered the job and began my career as a bilingual teacher.

During my ten-year teaching career, I taught every grade from Kindergarten through sixth, but I spent most of my years teaching fourth grade. I was assigned to several split classes where I taught two grade levels in one classroom. My organizational skills came in particularly handy there. I loved my students and focused on empowering them. I considered myself to be more of a facilitator of learning rather than a presenter of knowledge. With my real knack for creating engaging learning experiences for my class, I focused on showing my students how to use technology as a resource for learning as well as a way to synthesize knowledge and to share that knowledge with others. As a result, the school district administrators acknowledged my abilities and encouraged me to share my teaching strategies with other staff members. I began teaching technology and engaged learning workshops after school and also presented at regional and national educational conferences.

Nurturing my students as individuals was extremely important to me. By drawing on their strengths, I focused my lesson and activity planning on being supportive of their skills, talents, and interests. I completely despised state assessments and having to "teach to the test." I felt this kind of teaching was a waste of time and resources for my students and for me! I refused to spend too much time prepping my students for these exams. Being a teacher was a dream come true for me, and my enthusiasm and passion was evident to my students, colleagues, and administrators.

Janette being recognized as "Teacher of the Year" by Sam's Club and their executive team. (Addison, Illinois – 2001)

Head Over Heels

I met my husband, Joe, in college. We were officially introduced to each other the first weekend during freshmen orientation at Augustana College. We quickly became best of friends during the college years, but didn't actually start dating until after we both graduated. Joe grew up in Byron, Illinois (a small community two hours west of my hometown of Schaumburg), and after graduation he moved to the Chicago suburbs for a job opportunity. Since he was new to the area, he would call me to see if I wanted to catch a movie or have dinner with him.

This went on for a few months, and our friendship grew deeper. He would pick me up at my parents' house on a Saturday night, and we would hit the town. I remember one night as I was waiting for him to arrive, my mother asked with great curiosity, "So, are you dating Joe now?" I completely denied this to be true and said we were "just friends." My mom shook her head and said we had a strange relationship. I suppose to those on the outside we did!

One night while we were out with a bunch of our friends at a nightclub, something changed for me. I can remember Joe being surrounded by a few pretty girls. They were all laughing and flirting with him, and I just couldn't take it! I was overcome by jealousy and realized my feelings for him had gone to the next level. I had fallen head over heels in love. In my mind, I said, "Game over, ladies! Move out of the way! He's mine!" Before we knew it, Joe and I were engaged and planning our wedding. Joe and I laugh about not being able to remember our first date, and we proudly tell our story of how we were best friends before we were husband and wife.

Joe and Janette during the dating years (1996)

Joe and I were married on October 11, 1998 in a little neighborhood church on a beautiful, picture-perfect autumn day. Within four years of marriage, we bought our first house and soon decided it was time to start our family. In a short amount of time, we were delighted to be expecting our first child.

Joe and Janette's wedding portrait (Schaumburg, Illinois - October 11, 1998)

Before we were married, Joe and I had discussed how we both felt the importance of me staying home with our children to raise them. I felt the next step for my life was to be a housewife just as my mother did for my brother and me. So, I took a year off from teaching and stayed home with our son, as that was something really important to us. That is what my mom did, and she was a successful woman in my eyes.

Our son, Joey, was born in September of 2002. I absolutely loved having a baby in the house. I enjoyed my new role as mommy and loved taking care of our baby boy. I felt like this was what I was meant to do and why I was here on earth. People would tell me that I was just glowing, and that motherhood suited me well!

During that year, we found that it was difficult to pay our bills and get ahead financially without my steady paycheck and benefits. Joe was self-employed, and we were dealing with the expense of private health insurance and the ebbs and flows of his commission-based work. It was very stressful for me, and I yearned for more stability in our finances.

Joe and Janette as new parents with their son Joey and dog Rudy. (Glen Ellyn, Illinois – 2002)

I also found myself missing my career as a teacher. So, when Joey was about to turn one, I went back to teaching full-time. I quickly realized that being a working mother was quite stressful, and I really missed spending my days with my little boy. With the demands of my teaching job and the guilt I was feeling being away from our son, I felt that I was falling short of my own expectations as a wife, mother, and teacher.

To our surprise, in November of that school year, we discovered that we had another baby on the way! The combination of guilt, stress, and hormones made for a very long school year. Even though Joey was cared for by a wonderful sitter (our friend from church, Joyce Daniels) in her home, I cried almost every day having to leave him and go to work. After many discussions, Joe and I decided that I would take another year of maternity leave to stay home again when our daughter was born. At the end of the school year, I packed up my classroom belongings and headed home again to await the arrival of our daughter. I was relieved and excited to be a stay-at-home mom again.

Chapter 3

A Rainbow of Hope

Our daughter Jianna was born in early July, 2004. The delivery went extremely well, and the next day we were almost set to go home so we could celebrate the Fourth of July with our new bundle of joy! We were just an hour or so away from being discharged from the hospital when the unthinkable happened. Joe was holding her in his arms, and as we were talking he looked down at her and noticed that her color looked strange. He anxiously asked me if she looked alright, and when I noticed that her face was blue, we frantically called in the nurse. The medical staff whisked her away and told us that we were not going anywhere.

Joe and I waited in terror wondering what was going on and did not realize this was just the beginning of a long emotional experience for us. Joe went out to the store to buy me a robe and some magazines since I would be staying at the hospital longer than we had anticipated. While he was gone, I was visited by the neonatologist, Dr. Fisher. He explained that he was going to do a series of tests on our baby, including a spinal tap, and he asked me to sign the consent forms. I could not get a hold of Joe on his cell phone, so I signed the papers and sobbed until he came back.

After several hours and no conclusive test results, they brought us in to see Jianna in the Neonatal Intensive Care Unit. All I could do was cry seeing her lying in the incubator with wires taped all over her body and needles stuck in her little arms. I knew she was in good hands, but the separation anxiety I was feeling was agonizing. I just wanted her with me, and I pleaded to stay extra days in the hospital because I could not bear the thought of leaving without her. The nurses found an extra room for me to stay in for a couple of days, but eventually they needed that room for another patient.

I remember that day as if it were yesterday. I was so disappointed to be walking out of the hospital without our baby, and we were scared to pieces that we just might lose her. Joe was staying so strong, keeping in his emotions, but I knew it was killing him inside. He held me as we exited the hospital and walked to the car. It was a rainy and dreary day, and I kept thinking, "Why us?" As we were driving away, I couldn't take my eyes off of the hospital feeling as though we were abandoning our baby. Just then a rainbow appeared over the hospital, and I remember feeling as though it was a sign from God that she would be OK. It was our rainbow of hope.

Janette and Joe visiting their newborn daughter in the Neonatal Intensive Care Unit with their son Joey (Northwest Community Hospital, Arlington Heights, Illinois - July 2004).

We spent the next two weeks shuttling back and forth from the hospital to visit her. I would call the NICU staff early every morning hoping and praying for a good report and news that we could take her home. Her diagnosis was apnea and acid reflux. For some unknown reason, she would just stop breathing in her sleep. Her treatment was caffeine to keep her stimulated enough to keep breathing.

After a couple of weeks (which seemed like years), we finally received the news that we could take her home. This was exciting yet terrifying at the same time. Jianna came home with a breathing and heart monitor so an alarm would sound if she stopped breathing and so the doctor could monitor her from a distance. Joe and I were trained in infant CPR so we could be prepared if she had another episode. We called her our "Starbuck's Baby," as I had to give her a dose of caffeine each morning. The caffeine made her irritable, so she cried all the time. I hated not being able to comfort her, so I just held her and rocked her all day long.

After a few months, she finally outgrew the apnea and acid reflux and things were back on track! I was enjoying my life as a stay-at-home mom with our two children. All the while, the stress of not having steady income was keeping me up at night. Some months were fantastic financially, but others yielded no income. It was hard to keep a budget with the ebbs and flows, and we found ourselves depending on credit cards. We were yearning for a new opportunity that would help us turn our situation around for the better.

Chapter 4

On a Wing and a Prayer

J oe's long-time business friend (Ed Downey) approached him with a new business opportunity in 2004. Ed and Joe had worked together for a different company in the financial industry a couple of years back, and then they both went their separate ways. Ed was achieving great success in his financial firm and talked to Joe about how he had added a tax practice as a way to generate more financial business. Both Joe and I were really excited to hear more, and I felt this spark of hope for a more stable financial future for our family.

Joe started working in Ed's firm to learn this new business model. Once Joe was doing well enough, Ed approached him about branching out and starting his own business. We were really excited and looked into available sales territories. There weren't any open in Illinois, so we started to consider moving to Arizona, which was wide open at the time.

We had family living in Arizona and had honeymooned there. During our visits, we developed a great fondness for the beautiful scenery and warmer weather. In addition, my parents were thinking about retiring in Arizona, so we felt it would be an exciting move all in all. It would be a new adventure for our family and a new opportunity for success.

*A picture of the office building where Joe and Janette established
Gleason Tax Advisory Group, LLC (Surprise, AZ 2005)*

We sold our house in Illinois within a couple of months and headed west with the kids, both on blind faith and on a wing and a prayer. We were really determined to make it work. We had no doubt in our minds that we could make this business model succeed for us. Joe had been flying back and forth to Arizona to find office space and get a lay of the land. We had money in savings from Joe's income and from the sale of our house. We also had a stack of credit cards to fall back on if need be. In April of 2005, Gleason Tax Advisory Group, LLC was born, and we prepared our new office to service the residents of the retirement communities in the West Valley.

At the time, it was very popular in the financial industry to host educational seminars for retirees. Every month we did mass direct mailings to fill up our workshops, which we held at expensive steakhouses. Joe would present his seminar and then invite attendees to schedule an initial consultation. A certain percentage of people always wanted to meet with him, and some of those people became clients. The majority of the attendees, however, did not become clients. We let them walk out the door without any further communication. Each month we were spending thousands of dollars on marketing, but thankfully it was working. The revenue started rolling in!

We also started building our tax practice. We built up our database by offering discounted tax preparation services for seniors – at a cost of only forty-nine dollars. Once they came in for taxes, we would wow them with our service and work to convert them into financial clients. Within a year, we were so successful that we qualified for incentive trips and won trips to Cabo San Lucas, St. Maarten, and Lake Tahoe. Our client base grew in a very short period of time. It was exhilarating to have such immediate success – the system we had implemented was working!

Joe and Janette at an awards banquet for a Top Producers incentive trip in Lake Tahoe (June 2006)

Chapter 5

Surprise!

When we first started the business in April of 2005, I helped Joe by being his administrative assistant. I worked from home until the office space was ready, and then I came into the office to work part-time. The children were being cared for by a neighborhood nanny, and it seemed like a good balance for me. I was able to help and support Joe, but I was also able to enjoy time being a mom. My experience working in office settings throughout high school and college helped me manage and run the operations of our new business.

After a few months, we decided that it was time to hire our first employee. We hired an office manager, and I took on the role of financial processor. I playfully joke about that being "just in time." As we were in the process of building a house, we moved into a rental home in the city of Surprise, and then we got quite a surprise: our third baby was on the way – unexpected, but quite a delight. I realized I would need to take some time off, again, to be home with the children and raise the baby.

Upon finding out this baby way on the way, I was also really concerned about the likelihood of her having apnea as our first daughter did. I asked every doctor I saw about the probability of that happening, because it had been so traumatic for us. They told us that the probability of it happening again would be like lightning striking twice. I was somewhat relieved but still fairly worried.

Because of the horrible morning sickness I was experiencing (all-day sickness in fact), I could barely move off of the couch for fear of getting sick. Joey and Jianna loved all things Nickelodeon at the time, so even today when I hear Dora the Explorer or the Laurie Berkner Band, I get that sick to my stomach feeling! It was all I could do to keep it together throughout the day, and I was feeling guilty again. I wanted to have more energy to play with my children and to help Joe with the business, but my stomach and energy level had other plans for me!

By the time we moved into our brand new home, we had lived in four different houses within a span of one and a half years – from the house in Illinois, to our first house in Arizona, to a temporary rental home while our new house was being built, to our brand-new home. Our bills were piling up which caused us to feel strained financially. Since we were self-employed, our health insurance was minimal and didn't include maternity coverage. We were paying for the care and delivery of the baby out of our pockets, which was extremely expensive. I was anxious about that, particularly because I wasn't working. I was praying that there wouldn't be any complications.

I absolutely loved our new house, and we were settling in nicely. We made friends with the neighbors and enjoyed watching the kids play outside with their new friends. The business was doing well, and we began to furnish our home and enjoyed entertaining our friends and family. I was in full-on nesting mode preparing for the arrival of our new baby.

Chapter 6

Lightening Strikes Again!

One morning, when I was 35 weeks along, I began having contractions. I started getting things ready for me to go to the hospital. The baby's due date was in November, and it was only early October. In case of a false alarm, I didn't want to disturb Joe at the office. We had loaded our marketing for the beginning of the month, so he could take time off when she was born. He was holding several seminars at the time and conducting many appointments. I did not want to bother him during the middle of the day, so he could focus on generating business.

I packed up my overnight bag and put Joey and Jianna in the minivan. I remember stopping to pump gas in our van and having to take a break for a couple of contractions. I dropped the kids off with my parents and anxiously headed to the hospital. The doctor advised me that because I was only 35 weeks along, he was not going to stop the labor, but he wasn't going to help it along, either. Well, very soon after I arrived at the hospital, Jillian was indeed on the way.

I waited until I was sure we were having the baby before I called the office and spoke with our office manager. Joe was in an appointment with prospects at the time, and she knocked on the door and told him what was happening. I can only imagine that the look on his face was priceless! The lovely couple meeting with Joe was very understanding, and they urged him to go to the hospital right away. They eventually became clients, and still talk about this story each year during their annual review with Joe!

Joe rushed to the hospital to join me. The doctors were a bit concerned because 35 weeks is considered premature. During the delivery, many nurses were on standby just in case the baby needed urgent medical attention. Jillian was born weighing in at a healthy 7 pounds, 5 ounces with no complications. What a relief!

Because of the medical costs, we planned on staying for only two days. I mentioned to the nurses that our first daughter had apnea and asked them to keep a sharp eye on Jillian. I sent her into the nursery while I slept for my peace of mind.

When Jillian was one day old, I was feeding her, and the nurse noticed her color change. She immediately swept her out of my arms and took her to the Neonatal Intensive Care Unit. All I could think was, "Here we go again." It was just heartbreaking. Lightning had struck us a second time.

Once again, we wanted to be with our new baby. Once again, we couldn't do that. Fortunately, we were surrounded by angels. The nurses and doctors took wonderful care of Jillian. We discovered that because she was premature, she

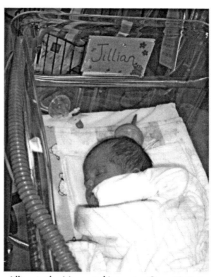

Jillian in the Neonatal Intensive Care Unit at Del E. Webb Hospital, (Sun City West, AZ)

lacked the coordination to drink, swallow, and breathe at the same time. Jillian also suffered from acid reflux, so she was treated with medication to reduce the pain she was experiencing.

I was able to stay for one extra day, but Jillian had to stay in the Neonatal Intensive Care Unit for a couple of weeks. Before we were allowed to take the baby home, we had to take a refresher course in infant CPR. It was so scary to think we might need to perform CPR on our newborn. It took a couple of weeks for her to stabilize. We spent those weeks traveling back and forth to the hospital to see our baby girl.

Once we brought her home, we had to watch her like a hawk. Anytime I fed her the lights had to be on, because it was important for me to be able to see the color of her skin.

Jillian's first day home with her sister Jianna and brother Joey (Surprise, Arizona – 2006)

The countless times I saw Jillian's face color change to a dusky blue, I would have to pinch her foot. This would startle her awake so that she would start to breathe again. I can remember one time Jillian had turned so blue that I placed her on the floor and got ready to do CPR thinking, "Oh God, this is it!" I pinched her foot really hard, and she started breathing on her own again. It was absolutely terrifying. I picked her up, held her against my chest, and burst into tears.

I was one stressed-out mom. Our son was almost four, our first daughter was two, and Jillian was an infant. They were all in diapers. I was still trying to help Joe with his business, as well, by doing accounting, payroll and some marketing for him. I love my children, and I have no regrets that I stayed home to take care of them, but day in and day out, I had to deal with diapers, keep the kids behaved, and maintain the household chores. It was incredibly difficult, and quite frankly, exhausting!

My mom was such a great mother and housewife, and I wanted to be just like her. Our house growing up was always immaculate. She had a homemade meal on the table every night. I thought that was what I should be doing. Unfortunately, I was giving so much to everyone around me that I wasn't doing anything for myself. I felt as if I had lost a piece of myself. I had been such a successful teacher, and I did not think it was possible to ever get that back again.

There are so many things I enjoyed about motherhood when the kids were little. I loved tending to the children, playing games and singing songs, washing their clothes, and even keeping their rooms tidy. I spoiled my babies by letting them fall asleep while I held them and doting on them every chance I had. I loved getting them ready to go on outings, like for a picnic in the park or a trip the library. I feel so blessed with the three wonderful children we have. It was just that I always believed that there had to be something more for me; something that would challenge my mind and give me a sense of purpose.

It was about this time that I realized I was in the beginning stages of depression. Why couldn't I have it both ways? I wanted to be "Mom," and it was too difficult for me to work outside of the home. So I gave up on my ambitions to pursue a career. We were also about to find out something about our son that would significantly change our lives.

Janette's family on Father's Day. (Surprise, Arizona - June 2007)

Part Two

FACING AUTISM
HEAD ON

Chapter 7

Red Flags

In 2006, we discovered that Joey had an autism spectrum disorder. Looking back, I realize the signs were always there with Joey. I just did not recognize them.

Here were some of the "red flags" we missed:

- Performs repetitive movements, such as rocking, spinning or hand-flapping
- Develops specific routines or rituals and becomes disturbed at the slightest change
- May be fascinated by details of an object, such as the spinning wheels of a toy car, but doesn't understand the "big picture" of the subject
- May be unusually sensitive to light, sound and touch
- Does not engage in imitative or make-believe play
- May have odd food preferences, such as eating only a few foods, or craving items that are not food, such as chalk or dirt
- May perform activities that could cause self-harm, such as headbanging

- Doesn't speak or has delayed speech
- Seems to prefer playing alone; retreats into his or her own world
- Doesn't ask for help or request things

~ www.mayoclinic.com

As far back as I can remember when Joey was a baby, he would love to watch the ceiling fan. His eyes were fixed on the constant circular movement of the blades. This fascination with spinning objects continued as he grew, especially with wheels. All he wanted to do was spin the wheels on his toy cars and trains repeatedly. During outings in his stroller as a toddler, he would insist on turning the stroller upside down so he could spin those wheels.

He did not play with toy cars the way other little boys do. He compulsively spun the wheels over and over. We simply didn't have any reason to recognize this as a sign of autism. He was so intelligent, and his cognitive level was extremely high. By the time he was sixteen months old, he had taught himself to recognize the entire alphabet and the sounds of each letter by playing a computer game. We were such proud parents, and as he was our first, we didn't have another child to compare him with developmentally. We did not realize his behaviors were not "normal." We just assumed he was brilliant!

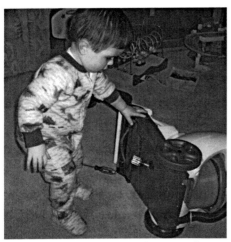

Joey at age 1 1/2 turning over the carpet cleaner to play with the wheels (Glen Ellyn, Illinois 2004)

Preoccupation with objects is another sign of autism. When he was a toddler, Joey had a preoccupation with trains. He went through a phase where he played with Thomas the Train all day long. He knew the name of every train in existence, and pushed his toy trains around, lined them up, and talked about them non-stop. He seems to go in stages with his pre-occupations and during his life he has become attached to all sorts of objects (Uno Wild Cards, gears, plastic caps, and Legos, to name a few).

Resistance to change is another red flag for autism, and this seems to be the most difficult part of autism for us to this day. I nursed Joey for the first thirteen months of his life. I did not introduce a bottle until he was a couple of months old, and he simply would not take it. It was hard for me to leave him

Joey at age 1 playing with his favorite toy. The gears would spin and light up. He brought this toy with him everywhere. (Glen Ellyn, Illinois 2004)

even for a short amount of time. I would have to schedule everything just perfectly. It felt like I always had to be home because he wouldn't take a bottle.

At the age of four, Joey still wasn't potty trained. I was at the end of my rope having three children in diapers. I tried EVERYTHING! I introduced incentive charts with stickers. I tried bribing him with toys. I sat on the bathroom floor with him for hours – days, even – trying to train him. It wasn't that he didn't want to use the potty; he just could not do it. I remember times where he would sit on his training potty for hours, and sometimes even fall asleep there. It was at the time when he turned four that I realized something had to be wrong. I was a teacher. I was an expert at reinforcing behavior, and I just couldn't get him to do this. I knew deep down that there must have been a reason to explain why potty training was so difficult for him.

I remember a day so vividly when Joey was four years old. I was just so fed up with the emotional and behavioral struggles with him day after day. I had so much anger building up inside of me. I do not recall what he did that day (he probably hit or threw something at one of his sisters), but I do remember that I sent him to his room for a time out. My insides were raging. As he was walking up the stairs, he looked back at me and made direct eye contact. I could see in his eyes that he was asking me for help. He was telling me, "Mommy, I can't help this.

I need help from you because I don't know what I'm doing. I just need your help." It was at that moment I realized I had to do something. I had to find out what was wrong and find out how to fix it. It was an impactful moment that I will never forget.

The Curse of Autism

Every child with autism is different. We are fortunate that Joey is on the high-functioning side of the spectrum. For our family, the most difficult times have to do with his resistance to change and difficulty making transitions in his life.

Each time we moved into a new home, it caused such emotional trauma to Joey. He just could not understand why his things were going into a new house. During one of our moves, Joey feel asleep on the couch while the movers were taking all of the furniture out into the truck. He awoke to an empty living room and just fell to pieces. It breaks my heart to think about how traumatic these moves were for him. He would get so upset that he would collapse into an emotional meltdown, and we couldn't comfort him.

The transition from home to school each day was always an adventure with Joey. I would never know what I was going to be up against each morning. He had such a difficult time making the transition from our minivan into the school. You might be thinking this is crazy, but that slight change in his routine daily could set him off into a downward spiral. There were many times when he would climb over his seat into the back hatch of the van and hide there for hours. His teachers, the aides, and administrators would come outside to coax him into school, but many times to no avail.

One day two teachers and I actually dragged him in through the front door, he fell on the floor crying, and I snuck out so he would not see me. That was the one and only time that happened. I went home and cried because of the gut-wrenching pain and guilt I felt. The next day I told the school we would never approach this situation in that way ever again, and they agreed. So many days enduring hours of getting him into the school, I would come home so wiped out emotionally that I was done for the day. I couldn't clean, work, or run the errands I had planned out for that day.

Vacations are also very difficult for Joey. Where a normal child gets excited about school breaks like Christmas Vacation or Spring Break, they are really hard for Joey. He used to get so upset in preschool and early elementary school that he would bang his head over and over on the inside of the window of our van and throw his shoes at me while I was driving the days leading up to a school break. He was not able to tell me when things bothered him, and it was so difficult for him to deal with the upcoming change in his schedule.

One year I was taking down our Christmas tree, and Joey became extremely upset to find it gone once he got home from school. He dropped down into the chair and cried for hours. Joe and I learned to constantly prepare him for any upcoming transitions, and that helped him cope better with changes in his life. We have to walk a very fine line though, making sure we tell him at the right time. If we tell him too early, he stays up at night worrying.

Joey's sisters have endured so much having a brother with autism. From getting hit in the head with a toy, to getting pushed down, to having to leave an event early because Joey needed to go, they have been troopers. I believe they're angels sent from heaven. God could not have chosen better sisters for him. They are wonderful, kind little girls that have learned how to help him. They are so patient, and they protect him unconditionally (Well, most of the time! They are siblings and have their moments!).

Children with autism can also suffer from sensory issues. Things happening in the environment that most of us can easily deal with, like loud noises, bright lights and lots of people, can be really difficult for autistic children.

For example, one day we took our family to a Diamondback's baseball game. My husband was so excited to share the love of baseball with his children. It was simply too difficult for Joey. There were so many people, so much noise, and so many bright lights that Joey and I ended up sitting in a hallway where it was very quiet and still. I sat there with him on the dirty floor watching him enjoy some popcorn and a soft drink. Not my idea of a good time at the ballpark! It's disappointing as a parent. You want to be able to share the same things that other families enjoy. Most of these things are simply too difficult for a child like Joey to handle.

Joey is also very sensitive to touch. For instance, he can only wear soft fabrics because something rough can physically hurt his skin. I used to get really frustrated before I understood this problem and forced him to wear button-down shirts or cute little ties. I have learned that a nice polo makes for a very handsome boy, no matter what the occasion! Joey was a ring bearer in his uncle's wedding, and we smile at the pictures of

Joey as a ring bearer with his little sister, Jianna, at their Uncle Tadd's wedding. Note the sneakers! (Joliet, Illinois – 2005)

him with his tuxedo shirt unbuttoned and wearing his sneakers! "Be flexible" is our motto!

He also has sensory issues with machinery like vacuum cleaners—anything that makes a loud noise. I always have to warn him or do things when he isn't around. Fire drills at school terrify him because they are so loud. An occupational therapist explained this very well to me during one of his evaluations. We were sitting in the room, and the therapist asked me if I could hear the copier running in the nearby reception area. I took me a moment of focus to hear it. The therapist said that Joey couldn't tune out unimportant sounds in his environment and that all sounds are equally loud to him, which can get overwhelming and simply too hard to bear.

When Joey was a toddler, he loved the Australian singing group The Wiggles. During his Wiggles phase, he watched their shows and would sing and dance with them every day. When we heard they were coming to Chicago, we bought tickets to go see them. I was so excited to bring him there. I have to admit that when they came onstage toot-toot chugging in their Big Red Car, I got teary eyed! Joey, however, spent the entire time underneath his chair because it was too much for him. The loud music, the bright lights, and the crowds of people overwhelmed him. He never again watched The Wiggles. It was too traumatic.

Normal things that make most kids happy are just not fun for Joey. When he was about a year old, I took him to Mommy and Me classes thinking he would love playing with the other kids and dancing to the upbeat music. Instead, he spent the entire time in the corner hiding away from the laughter and music. I would sit by him just wishing he would be "normal" like the other little ones joining in on the fun.

When Joey was in kindergarten, we decided to take the family on a cruise for our tenth wedding anniversary. We thought he would have so much fun going to the beach, eating a nice dinner every night, swimming in the pools, or even making another friend. We ended up spending most of our time riding the glass elevator. He loved hitting the buttons and go riding up and down, up and down, and up down. He would have stayed in there the entire time if we had let him! He also loved the arcade on the ship. There was a game that he played which gave out a variety of bouncy balls if he scored enough points. We came home with twenty-five of those balls and spent hundreds of dollars in that arcade to get them!

One day we were coming out of the arcade onto one of the decks of the ship. Joey resisted leaving, and Joe ended up having to carry him kicking and screaming back to the stateroom so he could settle down. I stayed on deck with the girls and my mom, who was with us on the cruise. I watched Joey kicking and screaming and yelling. He simply did not want to leave.

Another passenger observed Joey, and said very loudly to his family, "Did you see that kid? Did you see him? If that kid was mine, I'd throw him overboard!" I'm not usually a very outspoken person, but these comments stirred up such rage inside of me. He just didn't get it, and he wouldn't stop talking about it.

Finally I walked up to this man, and I said, "Sir, that boy is my son. Joey has autism. He is having a bad day, and your remarks are very painful." His face became pale, and he apologized. I wasn't trying to embarrass him. I just wanted him to understand that just because a kid is acting out doesn't mean he is bad or that his parents are negligent. You just never know. I sincerely hope he learned a lesson that day, and I pray he never makes that kind of hurtful mistake again.

Chapter 9

Finding Help

Finding help for Joey was no easy task. I asked for professional help often, but I had a hard time finding a doctor that knew enough about developmental issues to guide us in the right direction. When Joey was two years old, I went to his pediatrician concerned about the fact that he wasn't talking yet. The doctor said, "Oh, he's a boy. They develop later than girls. Don't worry. It will happen." I realized he was not going to help me, so I found another doctor that would advocate for him to receive speech therapy.

We were paired with a fantastic therapist who came to our home weekly to work with him. I sat and watched each and every lesson, and I continued the same exercises with him daily. Within a few months, Joey was speaking at his age level and his services were discontinued. I was so proud of him, and I felt so relieved with his new ability to communicate with us using words. I did not know that this was the first of many battles I would have to fight for our son.

Potty training was another issue. At his four year old well-check, I pleaded with his pediatrician to help me potty train him. She first prescribed a laxative, and although I knew it wasn't the answer, I gave it a try. After a couple of weeks, I called the pediatrician's office again to tell her the laxatives were not working. After doing her research, she came back with a "solution" for this dilemma. She suggested locking him in his bedroom and only letting him out when he asked to use the potty. My immediate reaction was, "Absolutely not! I would never lock him in his room." I could not believe this kind of recommendation would be advised by a health professional. Needless to say, it was time to find another pediatrician again.

I kept trying different strategies until I finally found the one that worked. I called my brother-in-law, Tadd, and asked him if he would pretend he was Spider-Man when Joey finally had success going on the potty. With Tadd on stand-by and a stash of cupcakes, candles, and party blowers on hand, I told Joey he could call his hero Spider-Man when he "went" for the first time. After a few days of my proposition and some major cheerleading on my part, Joey did it! We had the best celebration ever! We lit candles, ate our cupcakes, drank our fruit punch, sang and did a happy dance. Then Joey had the most wonderful conversation with Spider-Man, who told him how proud he was and that Joey was now officially a big boy. That was that. No more pull-ups, no laxatives, no accidents - just a very happy mommy indeed!

One night we heard that our pastor and his wife from Illinois, Brandon and Christy Woosley, recently discovered their two boys had autism spectrum disorders, so I gave her a call to see if I could find any answers. Christy explained what she was going through, and it was amazing for me to hear the similarities. We spent hours talking on the phone, and I was amazed at her knowledge, dedication, and drive to help her boys. I no longer felt so alone. I took lots of notes during our calls. Then I began to research and read a definition of Asperger's Syndrome on the internet. When I read the description, a wave of terror fell from my head to my feet. I was reading about Joey. Tears flowed out of my eyes as I looked at the computer screen. They were tears of sadness, but in a way, tears of relief as well.

Christy advised that I take him to see a developmental pediatrician for an evaluation. We scheduled an appointment for him at the Melmed Center in Scottsdale, Arizona and had him evaluated. They were able to give us the answers for which we had been searching for so long!

I also took him to our public school district's preschool screening. I was in the third trimester of my pregnancy with Jillian, and found myself so exhausted by the end of the screening event. After a couple of hours, a speech therapist approached me while Joey was rolling around on the floor crying. She asked me if he lined up his toys and if he has trouble sharing with others, and some other questions I don't recall. When I answered yes to all of her questions, she took my hand and guided me to sign up for further testing. Her touch lifted hundreds of pounds of stress off of my shoulders. After a complete evaluation, they found he exhibited symptoms of social delay and some other developmental issues, and they allowed him to enter their special education preschool program. It was there that I learned how to prepare him for events and put plenty of structure in his day.

I would use what I referred to as the "one-two-three's." If we were going out, I would say, "Joey, first we are going to the bank, second we are going to the store, and third we are going to Grandma's house." I would repeat the series of events again. "Joey, first we are going to the bank; second we are going to the store; and third we are going to Grandma's house." After we went to the bank, I would tell him, "Okay, Joey. We went to the bank. Now we are going to the store, and then we are going to Grandma's house." Once I started doing that and he observed me following through with my promises, he could predict what was going to happen during his day. His teachers also helped by making him some calendars and charts. That way we could prepare him for breaks and other changes in his routine.

I worked really hard to get Joey services through the Department of Developmental Disabilities. After months of evaluations and interviews, we were thankfully able to secure services for him. He started intensive therapy starting at the age of five, including speech therapy, physical therapy, music habilitation, and occupational therapy. These interventions were very successful. We saw great results after his therapists began working with him. He met many of the goals they set for him very quickly.

I also believe that God sent angels to look after Joey. When he was going into Kindergarten, I was really scared that they would remove him from special education and put him in a regular classroom without any support. He was doing well at preschool, but I was concerned about him entering Kindergarten. I started looking for all options for him. We returned to the Melmed Center for additional answers and guidance. It was at that time that we did more assessments, and he was diagnosed with high-functioning autism, sensory integration disorder, developmental coordination disorder, tic disorder, and anxiety.

I took this documentation back to the public school. They conducted their own assessments and called a meeting to discuss their final decision. The day we had this meeting, I said a prayer in the car before I went into the school, asking God to open those doors that needed to be opened and to close those that needed to be closed. I needed guidance and answers for Joey. I walked into a room of 16 administrators, psychologists, therapists, and teachers. I was completely intimidated and felt blind-sided. They energy in the room was terrible, and their demeanor was cold.

Each staff member took turns presenting evaluation results, and the school psychologist informed me that they believed his disabilities would not affect his ability to learn or function in a regular classroom. His special education support was denied. I explained to them that not being able to get him to walk into the classroom each day would seriously affect his ability to learn. They still denied him any special education support. Even though I could have fought the school's decision with proof of his autism diagnosis, I knew that those doors were being closed.

We looked into finding another option for him. We found a nearby charter school, and they accepted him with open arms. Thankfully, his Kindergarten teacher, Mrs. Raby was an angel. She took such good care of him. Since she had never had an autistic child in her classroom before, she conducted research over the summer to prepare for him. She allowed Joey to visit her and see his new classroom before school even started. Witnessing her patience and gentleness helped reassure me that he was going to be in good hands.

We talked about his sensory problems, and she developed a simple signal for him to show her when he needed some quiet time. During a noisy assembly, he only needed to place his hand on top of his head, and she would allow him to go back to his classroom. Every day when I picked him up from school, she gave me an update of how his day had gone. I was so grateful that she took him under her wing and cared for him so much.

That year we also found a great habilitation and respite provider named Miss Jennifer who came to our home and helped me with Joey. She was responsible for assisting him with achieving several goals including community safety, self-help, and life skills. Every single weekday morning Miss Jennifer would come to our house early in the morning to help me get him ready for school. When she would arrive, I had a pot of coffee ready for us to share. We would talk for a bit and then prepare ourselves mentally for the difficult challenge of waking Joey, getting him dressed and ready, and then taking him to school. She returned many afternoons to spend time with Joey so I could take my daughters to dance class and run errands. Jen is now a close family friend and someone our family is so fortunate to have in our lives.

Joey's peers also so innocently supported him. For instance, whenever the music teacher would come into the classroom, Joey would go hide under a table. The other kids at the table would go under with him, and say, "Hey, Joey, it's okay. Come on up." At that point, I realized these were all angels sent to support him and help him get to where he is today.

Chapter 10

The Blessings of Autism

Even though it can be a very lonely and heartbreaking life raising a child with autism, we have experienced miracles as he progresses and reaches new milestones. I have learned to cherish the little things. Everything happens on "Joey's Time" and when Joey is ready. If we push him too hard about anything, he resists and shuts down. We have found it is best to let go, wait patiently, and allow Joey to progress at his own pace.

As a toddler, we were on a first name basis. Joey called me "Nette" and he called my husband "Joe." That was what he heard us call each other, and he just could not grasp the concept that we were "Mommy and Daddy." We would laugh it off as being cute, but deep down I felt disappointed and embarrassed at times. I'll never forget the very first time Joey called me Mommy. For so many parents, that's their child's first word. It took me years to hear that from my son. I had to wait so long, but that moment completely melted my heart.

As his parent, I have learned to appreciate the little accomplishments he makes, like the first time he rode a bike. We bought him a bicycle and hoped to teach him how to ride it without training wheels, but he had no interest. One day he watched his little sister the first day she started riding her bike. A couple of weeks later he figured it out all by himself. We burst out with laughter to suddenly see him hop on his sister's bike and ride across the back patio with no training wheels! As Joey made the decision that he wanted to learn, then there was no looking back!

When he was in first grade, I still had to drop him off in the Kindergarten area of the school, because he was comfortable there with Mrs. Raby. It was not until Spring Break of first grade that he said, "Mommy, after Spring Break, I'm ready to be dropped off at first grade." This was a wonderful milestone for Joey. I said, "Okay, Joey. It's your time, and I'm so proud of you."

Joey has always had a hard time expressing his emotions. Saying good-bye, expressing sadness, and even saying "I love you" were difficult for him. We just accepted the fact that he could not share his emotions. Joey came up to me one day and said, "Mommy, I love you. I don't know what I would ever do without you," and he gave me a hug. He was seven years old at the time. I waited so long to hear something like that from my son. It was very heartfelt and thoughtful, and hearing those words made an everlasting impact on my life. I feel lucky to have that memory, regardless of how long it took to hear it.

It's the little things with Joey that make the biggest difference in my life. He has made me a better person. I am more patient, more compassionate, stronger, and wiser because of him. He is a blessing to our family.

✦ Part Three ✦

ENTER
INFUSIONSOFT

Chapter 11

When the Music Stopped Playing

In 2007, things were coming to a head for me, and not in a good way. Our bills were piling up. We were trying to get our small business to work. All three of our kids were still wearing diapers. I attempted going back to work full-time to help out financially, but I found that I wasn't making enough money with three kids in daycare. That was really stressful for me, especially since almost every penny I earned went to pay for their childcare. I also hated leaving my children each and every day. It was far too much for me to bear.

I was also internally struggling with the fact that we were dealt the autism card. I kept thinking, "Why us?" Being in the trenches on a daily basis with the emotional and behavioral issues that came along with autism was overwhelming. I felt resentful having to rearrange the structure of our lives to accommodate Joey's needs. I wished for a more normal way of life.

Joe's business had been fairly stable, and our marketing efforts had continued to bring in a somewhat steady stream of income for us. Because of the saturation of financial planners in our area, over time it became necessary for us to send out more direct mail pieces.

Unfortunately, we were getting less and less of a response each month. We were taught "marketing always pays," so we kept on with our direct mail and seminar marketing system.

In January of 2008, we invested approximately $15,000 in marketing. This was for direct mail advertising for seminars with fancy steak dinners. That month, we did not acquire any new clients or convert any new sales. The same thing happened again in February. We started using our line of credit from the business in order to pay our home and office bills. We were eating peanut butter sandwiches at home while we were feeding our prospects steak dinners. The marketing that we had depended on for so long stopped working. The music stopped playing, and we were left without a chair.

I felt I had no control over anything in my life.

That was when I found myself having anxiety attacks. I didn't want to pay thousands of dollars for marketing any longer. I didn't want to find any bills when I went to the mailbox. I didn't want a credit card company calling me harassing me about late payments. I found myself sneaking into the bathroom to have my anxiety attacks. After I shut the door, the attack would begin. My heart would start racing, and my stomach would tighten up. As I was overcome with fear, the shortness of breath would start. I'd breathe in and out in a frenzy, trying to get through the attack. Once it was over, I'd put a smile back on my face and continue with my day, trying to be the wife and the mom I thought I should be - and nobody knew this was happening.

I felt so helpless because I couldn't work. Joey needed me at home, and so did our girls. I tried getting some part-time jobs, such as being the Sunday School Superintendent at our church and dabbling in selling cosmetics through a network marketing company, but I failed miserably at keeping a good balance between home and work.

It really started bothering me that I couldn't help provide for my family. I began having these recurring dreams about being in water and drowning. In my dreams, I couldn't keep my head above water. Whether it was a pool or the ocean, these dreams kept coming back. It was really symbolic of being in financial distress. It felt as if we were at a poker game, and we were playing all of our chips every single month hoping we were going to win and get some money back. It was scary to think we could lose everything.

Along with the anxiety attacks, I started feeling really depressed. I was crying often from feeling totally helpless. I remember lying in bed one night and thinking about how difficult life had become. After I fell asleep, I was dreaming and a flash of light startled me awake. My heart was racing, and I was gasping for air. It was at that moment I realized I needed to change my thought process. I needed to stop feeling sorry for myself, stop feeling out of control, and stop feeling weak. I needed to be strong and supportive for my family, and I needed to be present. I knew I had to change my way of thinking completely.

This was the point where I resolved to take back control of my life.

That began my journey of healing. I started meditating and taking natural supplements. I was taking things day by day. One of the greatest lessons I learned was that the sun will always rise tomorrow. Whether or not I pay my bills, or whether or not we stay in business; the sun will always rise. I realized the most important thing was having my husband and my children. I became determined to resolve this internal struggle about who I should be and to find purpose in my life again.

Chapter 12

A Paradigm Shift

We had come to the point where we acknowledged our marketing system was no longer working. Something had to change. After all, the definition of insanity is doing the same thing over and over again expecting a different result. In January, our marketing failed. In February, our marketing failed. Had we used the same marketing in March, it most likely would have failed again, and we would have gone deeper into debt. It was time to change, and luckily I was soon introduced to the concept of email marketing.

At that time in our business, we did not even have a website. I did some research, and we subscribed to an email marketing system for financial planners. This company even set up a basic website for us. We then watched a special on PBS hosted by the IRA guru, Ed Slott. Joe had been to many of his trainings, believed in what he was doing, and was implementing many of his tax saving strategies with his clients. We decided to send an email blast to our database inviting them to watch that show on PBS. We were hoping they would see it as helpful and that it would drive them to want a consultation with Joe. The response was tremendous! They appreciated the show's content, and many scheduled an appointment to discuss these matters with Joe.

As a result, we ended up having the biggest one-time sale since we had been in business in Arizona. That was really exciting, and we realized we were on the right track!

 GLEASON TAX ADVISORY GROUP, LLC

Dear Janette,
Tonight is the last showing of Ed Slott's PBS special STAY RICH FOR LIFE. The feedback we have received regarding this informational program has been outstanding. Many of my clients have watched this program and are eager to implement Mr. Slott's tax and financial strategies. The response has been so overwhelming, and I urge you to tune in or set your DVR to record STAY RICH FOR LIFE.

Tune in to PBS channel 8 or set your DVR to view this program at the following times:
Saturday, June 12 at 12:30 am

 ED SLOTT'S STAY RICH FOR LIFE features all new information and Slott's inviting blend of in-depth, real-world research, humor, and detailed facts from the tax code to make financial planning accessible. In his new special, Slott presents practical explanations and proven guidelines including:

- How to move from "forever taxed" to never taxed
- The IRA account's "evil twin" - Uncle Sam
- History of the top tax rate - over 70% for most of the 20th Century
- How to crack the code - the tax code
- The "Amazing" ROTH IRA
- Ed's 5-step plan

A portion of the email invitation we created for Ed Slott's PBS special (June 2008)

A friend of ours named Steve Heideman suggested to us that if we intended to do a lot of email marketing, we should invest in a software program called Infusionsoft, a customer relationship management system that automated email marketing to your database (and so much more). It was Steve that encouraged Joe to think about how many sales he was leaving on the table by not following up with prospects and clients. Joe realized he did not have a system to follow-up and stay in touch with the thousands of leads we had acquired over the years.

So, with the revenue from our big sale, we invested in Infusionsoft. For the first couple of years that we had Infusionsoft, we were only skimming the surface of the software's capabilities. Joe knew it could do so much more, but since he was running a business, he did not have time to delve in and customize the software for our needs. We had this amazing tool at our disposal, but we weren't taking full advantage of it. My husband said it was like having a Ferrari sitting in our garage, but never taking it out for a drive! We just needed some extra help and guidance, or as it turned out, a certain turn of events that got us headed in the right direction.

Joe was utilizing the database for storing information about our prospects and clients, the calendar system for scheduling appointments, and the email module for sending email blasts to our entire database. We thought our messages were so important that everyone in our database wanted to hear what we had to say each and every time. Later we discovered there was a better method and that we could use Infusionsoft to send messages to a more targeted list. Our clients appreciated the regular communications from us, and we felt good about the results we were experiencing.

When market volatility hit, our financial planning business suffered. Our expenses kept rising, but Joe's commissions were being reduced. We found ourselves having to do more marketing while making less of a profit. The bills kept coming in, and each month we had to prioritize which ones we would pay. Infusionsoft had become a top priority of ours. We understood its potential and realized that we could potentially go out of business without it.

Joe and I felt as though were prisoners of our own business. We couldn't go on vacation, and we couldn't leave the daily operations of running our small business. We were not sure if we would be able to keep the "lights on" from week to week, and we began to feel so discouraged. This biggest pain Joe felt was worrying that he would not be able to continue serving his client base throughout their retirements as he had promised them.

It was a really tough time at that point, and truthfully, I just wanted to go home. I wanted to go back to Illinois, because I had grown to hate Arizona. I felt really alone. It seemed like every time we made friends, they'd move away for other job opportunities or other reasons. Joe really kept the faith, and I give him a lot of credit for that. We started our small business in order to have freedom, but instead we were feeling trapped with no way out. Then another unexpected turn caught us off guard.

Chapter 13

A Blessing in Disguise

In November of 2010, our office manager quit without warning. While she was the only employee at the time and with me being at home with the kids, this put us in quite a predicament. We realized it would be a slow period with the holidays coming up, so Joe asked me to come in and help out. While I was working, my mom and dad watched the kids so I could help interview, hire, and train a new employee who would start up in January to manage tax season.

I started playing around with Infusionsoft and learning everything possible about it. I realized we were just skimming the surface of the software's capabilities. I registered to watch their free training webinars. Jordan Hatch, the amazing Infusionsoft guru, was hosting educational webinars weekly, and I was sure to tune in every time to learn new ways to use the software! Infusionsoft also had this new Drag and Drop Email Builder that was really easy for me to use, and it made our communications with our contacts look so professional! I found myself looking forward to getting on the computer to try out something new.

One day I listened to an Infusionsoft webinar about Lifecycle Marketing. The hosts taught us about the seven stages each prospect should go through to maximize our marketing dollars, increase our sales, and help retain clients.

The stages of Lifecycle Marketing are as follows:

1. **Attract Traffic** – Use a variety of advertising methods to attract interest to your company (newspaper ads, signage, a website, social media, word of mouth, etc.).

2. **Capture Leads** – Have an offer so prospects will request to receive information from you (e-book, free consultation, coupon, quote, report, etc.) Use an opt-in such as a web form to collect their contact information (name, email, phone number etc.) to store in your database.

3. **Educate Prospects** – Deliver the information the prospect requested in a systemized way and educate them about your products and services.

4. **Convert Sales** – Keep in touch with the prospect until they are ready to buy from you. Have a system for converting the sale.

5. **Deliver and Satisfy** – Wow your new customer with great service and delivery of the product(s).

6. **Upsell Customers** – Provide opportunities to upsell to your new customers and to have them become a repeat customer in the future.

7. **Get Referrals** – Create a referral program so your satisfied customers have an incentive to refer their friends and family to you.

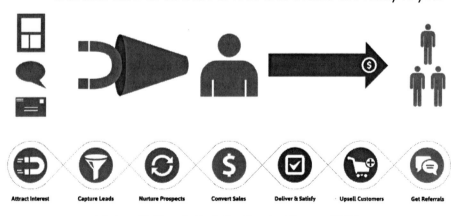

Infusionsoft's Lifecycle Marketing Flowchart (January 2010)

My background was in elementary education. I had no training in marketing or business – but it all made so much sense to me. At the end of the webinar, they gave us a worksheet with a column for each of the stages. I started filling in the worksheet with examples of what our current marketing methods were. Immediately, I saw these gaping holes. We were not educating and nurturing our prospects, and we had no formalized referral program.

I started concentrating heavily on the areas that needed work. I remember becoming so excited about what this software was doing for us. Joe actually nicknamed me "The Mad Scientist." He would come home from work after I had spent the day at home creating a new website, developing a follow-up sequence, or building a referral program, and I couldn't stop talking about all that happened that day. Every day I researched and worked on something new, and I couldn't wait to show Joe what I had done. I would even wake up in the middle of the night and head to the den to watch a tutorial and build something in the software.

 GLEASON TAX ADVISORY GROUP, LLC

The Ultimate Tax Planning Guide

Dear Janette Gleason,

Thank you for your interest in our guidebook.

You can now download your copy of The Ultimate Tax Planning Guide. Take a moment to read through the guidebook and learn about areas where you can potentially reduce your taxes!

We hope you find this 30+ page guide very informative!

As always, if you have any questions please feel free to call us at: **623-815-9100.**

Best wishes!

The Staff of Gleason Tax Advisory Group, LLC

The ULTIMATE Tax Planning Guide

Download The Ultimate Tax Planning Guide now by clicking on the attachment below:

📎 The Ultimate Tax Planning Guide.pdf

An email Gleason Tax Advisory Group, LLC sent out to existing tax clients to educate them about our tax planning strategies.

I began nurturing the prospects and clients that were already in our database. I created a monthly newsletter to send out to our list of contacts. I created an e-book called "The Ultimate Tax Planning Guide" and put it on our website as an opt-in. I also set up automatic birthday greetings for our financial clients and monthly offers to our tax clients.

I even made plans for Joe to host a series of webinars. The thought occurred to me that Joe could deliver the same message about retirement planning from his seminars on a webinar, and we wouldn't have to pay for the steak dinners! I sent an email invitation to our tax clients explaining what would be covered and how to sign up. We had about twenty people register for our very first webinar!

The lessons learned were:

#1– By nurturing the thousands of contacts already in our database, we could increase our sales while decreasing our marketing budget.

#2– We could get our message across in some innovative and exciting ways.

We said good-bye to seminar marketing FOREVER!

We didn't have much money in the budget to do advertising for our tax preparation that season. In the past, we had sent out postcards and placed ads in the local newspaper. I decided to try using a series of emails to market to our database. That year we booked over 800 tax appointments using only email marketing and were even on a waiting list! We ended up having to turn people away that year. What a relief it was not having to spend a dime on advertising. We also used a referral program that offered a ten-dollar gas card in exchange for referring a friend, and we acquired many new clients from this program.

That year we also increased our base price from $49 to $89 for a basic tax return. We started charging for add-on services (such as an additional state, extra schedules, or extensive research). Our revenue doubled, enabling us to start putting money back into the business. After about thirty days, we began seeing results. The business was growing. We felt tremendous pride for what we had accomplished in such a short amount of time. Even more, Joe felt great to have my support and involvement in his business.

Little did I know that my life was about to change forever.

The
Turning Point

During one of Infusionsoft's educational webinars, they mentioned a contest called the "Ultimate Marketer Contest." They were looking for the best new marketing plan among Infusionsoft customers willing to share their work and ideas. I thought, "I could be the next Ultimate Marketer! Look at what we've done!" so I printed out the contest's application. I also printed a copy of their logo (which was a golden trophy), wrote my name on it, and kept it on my desk for inspiration. I wanted to be the Ultimate Marketer more than anything. I poured my heart out as I filled in the answers. I identified our strategies in each phase of the Perfect Customer Lifecycle, attached the samples of our marketing pieces, created a flowchart, and shared our story. After I submitted my application, I kept it a secret. I didn't want to look silly for trying if I wasn't chosen as a finalist.

The Ultimate Marketer Contest advertisement that inspired Janette to enter the contest in 2011.

Within a couple of nerve-racking weeks, I received an email message from Nicole Shoots, the event coordinator at Infusionsoft. She informed me that I was one of their top eight finalists for the contest and said she wanted to ask me some additional questions. I was so excited! Just being recognized was enough – the fact that they even considered me was overwhelming, and I felt so proud of myself. Joe came home that evening, and I finally told him I entered the contest and that I was one of eight being considered as a finalist. Completely taken by surprise, he said, "What contest? You entered a contest?"

```
Hi Janette,
My name is Nicole and I am the event coordinator at Infusionsoft. In addition to coordinating
InfusionCon, I am also in charge of the Ultimate Marketer contest. First, I want to congratulate you
and let you know that you are one of our top 8 submissions!

We are meeting tomorrow to finalize the three finalists, but before we do I would like to ask a
couple more questions.
1. The (after Infusionsoft) revenue number you submitted, is that the revenue you grew since starting
with Infusionsoft?
2. How many full time employees are in your company?
3. How many part time employees?
4. How many contractors or virtual assistants does your company utilize?

Thank you so much for submitting to the contest. I look forward to hearing from you!

Nicole Shoots
```

The email message from Nicole Shoots asking Janette to clarify and answer some questions for the Ultimate Marketer Contest (2011)

Nicole called me a couple of days later to advise me that I was one of the top three finalists, and she invited me to make a presentation at their annual user conference in March (InfusionCon 2011). It was hard to contain my excitement on the phone with her, and as soon as we hung up, I laughed and cried. I called Joe to tell him the wonderful news - but then I thought, "Oh, crap! Now I have to speak in front of a thousand people! I had better buy myself a really nice dress and get to work on my presentation." I was so nervous the days leading up to the contest, but I felt a great sense of purpose. I was hoping my story would inspire others. I figured my message for the small business owners attending the conference had to be, "If a stay-at-home mom can do this, so can you!"

The first day of the conference finally arrived, and I attended by myself. Joe couldn't go because he was so bogged down with managing tax season. I was scared to pieces when I walked into the conference hall because there were so many people there. I went into the main room, and when I saw the huge stage from which I would be speaking the next day, my jaw dropped and almost hit the floor!

Upon arriving at the conference, I had never met even a single person there. The only person I knew was Infusionsoft's event coordinator, Nicole Shoots. I recognized Jordan Hatch's name because he facilitated the webinars and had taught me just about everything I knew about Infusionsoft! While at the conference, I was able to meet so many fascinating people – other business owners with an ambition for success, friendly Infusionsoft executives and employees, and vendors offering services I never knew existed.

I realized I was surrounded by experts – people who knew about API integrations, iPads, and iPhones. I had never seen an iPad before one of the conference attendees showed one to me. There were big time professional speakers there like the Secret Millionaire's James Malinchak and sales legend Brian Tracy. How humbling it was to know I was going to be speaking on the same stage as them! Then I met my competition for the Ultimate Marketer Contest: top-notch marketers Jermaine Griggs from Hear and Play Music, and Sean Kelly and Andy Mackensen from H.U.M.A.N. Healthy Vending. I was very honored to be among the ranks of such great talent.

I was scheduled to make my presentation the following day, first thing in the morning. Nicole chose names out of a hat, and I was up first! I was completely and utterly nervous. Joe really helped and encouraged me. In our preparation before the event, he said, "I'll do the introduction and talk about life before Infusionsoft. Then I'll bring you up for your part. When you start, I want you to just put it out there. Tell everyone who you are and that you're nervous. Once you get it out of the way, then you can go on."

As we were waiting for our turn, I was absolutely terrified. Joe went up first and did his part, and then it was show time! I told my story, did just as Joe recommended, and shared the work that I did. I gave it my all. Honestly, I don't know how it all came together. I do remember that it was the warmest and friendliest audience in the world. Throughout my presentation, I could see their smiles and hear their applause. There was laughter for my stories, and there were tears when I shared our struggles with autism.

When I was done, I couldn't believe what was happening - We were receiving a standing ovation! Joe and I walked off the stage and down the aisle together. That's a moment I'll never forget. Afterwards, women came up to tell me they too had children with autism and that they understood what I was going through. Men came up and told me how great it was that I was helping my husband with our family business. It was really exciting! I felt humbled and really proud that I was able to inspire others.

On the third day of the conference, they were to announce the winner of the contest towards the end of the day. As Joe and I stood on stage with the other finalists, the anticipation was intense! I felt like I was an American Idol contestant waiting for Ryan Seacrest to deliver my fate.

Janette during her Ultimate Marketer Presentation at InfusionCon 2011 (Phoenix, AZ – March 2011)

The winner was finally announced, and the well-deserving Jermaine Griggs of Hear and Play Music (www.hearandplay.com) was named the Ultimate Marketer of the Year. I didn't earn the title of Ultimate Marketer, but I won just the same. A new opportunity was born along with a new career. It was really just the beginning for me, and the best was yet to come!

Ultimate Marketers and Finalists at InfusionCon 2011 with Joe and Janette Gleason, Sean Kelly, Jermaine Griggs, Andy Mackenson, and Bob Britton (Ultimate Marketer Winner 2010).

Chapter 15

Onward
and Upward

After the Ultimate Marketer Contest, I continued learning about marketing with Infusionsoft with a spring in my step and a smile on my face. I attended all of their webinars, and I studied all of their tutorials. As a result, I was able to streamline all of the processes in Joe's business. We were able to automate repetitive tasks that our staff performed multiple times each day. I took the completely manual and redundant system for our tax appointment scheduling process and integrated it completely into Infusionsoft. Originally when a prospect called to schedule a tax preparation appointment, our administrative assistant would write all of their information on a paper form, enter that information into our database, and then hope we could remember to follow up with reminders. Now the process is completely computerized, saving us time and eliminating human error.

We customized a sales pipeline system to keep Joe's leads from falling through the cracks. Our existing tracking system consisted of file folders, memo pads, and sticky notes! We needed a more effective way to track our leads and follow-up with them more consistently. The process of meeting with a prospect for an initial consultation to their financial plan being fully implemented can take weeks, even months sometimes. Our eighteen-stage pipeline allows us to move prospects through the sales process and keep track of them on our dashboards (our Infusionsoft homepage). With each stage movement, a variety of tasks are completed for us automatically, such as sending a thank you card or following up with an email. This complex pipeline system helps us nurture our prospects, convert more sales, keep them informed during the entire process, and provide an exceptional welcome experience for our new clients.

Here are some of the stages currently included in our sales pipeline:

- New Opportunity
- Postponed
- Initial Consultation
- Research and Planning
- Recommendations Meeting
- Prepare Paperwork
- Signing Appointment
- Processing
- Document Delivery
- Closed/Won

Infusionsoft makes it easy for our company to roll out the red carpet for our new clients. When moved into the "Processing" stage, they are automatically sent a delicious box of brownies with a card that welcomes them to our family of clients. The head of household and spouse are both immediately added to our automated birthday greeting campaign when they enter the "Closed/Won" stage. Throughout the year, we invite our clients to client appreciation events and educational programs, and

An appreciation gift Gleason Financial Group, LLC sends to thank and welcome Joe's new clients (a customized card and scrumptious brownies)

Infusionsoft helps us with the event coordination and execution from beginning to end.

Once our business became completely systematized, I realized I could do this for other companies. I decided to branch out, and Gleason Consulting Group, LLC was founded. In December of 2011, I went to the Infusionsoft Certified Consultant's training for three days. Thankfully I ended up passing their grueling six-hour exam (I was shaking in my boots) and became one of only 100 people in the world to be certified by Infusionsoft at that time. Now I am an international business and marketing consultant with clients in Australia, Singapore, Canada,

Janette and the Infusionsoft Certified Consultants Class
(Gilbert, Arizona - December 2011)

Puerto Rico and, of course, the United States. I've worked with a wide range of businesses from a cleaning service to an improv comedy show.

I have been fortunate enough to get to know other small businesses owners and entrepreneurs in a wide variety of industries.

The following is a list of some types of clients I have served:

- Author
- Financial Advisor
- Realtor
- Marketing Consultant
- Improv Comedy Show

- Doctor
- Sports Equipment Retailer
- Interior Designer
- Massage Therapist
- Holistic Health Specialist

- Document Shredding Service
- Weight Loss Coach
- Cleaning Service
- Travel Agent
- Business and Life Coach
- Attorney
- Insurance Agent
- Tax Professional
- Real Estate Investor

During my first year as a consultant, I completed many Kickstart Coaching Sessions with new Infusionsoft customers to help them get up and running. My role was to help them get off to a fast start and to experience success with the software quickly. I helped them configure Infusionsoft with their business processes and get their databases imported. I taught them about the contact management, marketing, e-commerce, and referral modules in the software. During our coaching sessions, I helped them design marketing campaigns, and I taught them how to incorporate Lifecycle Marketing into their businesses, as well.

I love sharing the passion my clients feel for their businesses. It has been really rewarding for me and has been a great learning experience.

✳ Part Four ✳

MY LIFE AS A
MOMPRENEUR

Chapter 16

Two for the Price of One!

Over the past couple of years, I have been able to recognize my gifts as a consultant and the value I contribute to other small businesses. I see the importance of these gifts as they pertain to creating and executing a complete marketing plan for a client and helping a small business owner achieve the next level of success.

A WHOLE-BRAIN APPROACH

I incorporate a whole-brain approach when working with my clients. Generally speaking, most people either have a global mind or a linear mind. People with a global mind can see the big picture. They can theorize and put ideas together, but they don't know how to implement those ideas in a practical and detailed way. Those who have a linear mind (and know all the nuts and bolts) know how to implement, but they can't see the forest through the trees. They don't have the ability to execute with a strategic overall plan in mind. I'm unique in that I have both a global and a linear mind. As a huge benefit for my own businesses and for my clients, I can plan with the big picture in mind and also handle the practical side of a marketing project or business strategy. When hiring me, my clients get two for the price of one!

DEEP INSIGHT

As a consultant, I also have a really deep understanding of human nature. I'm a nurturer. It's a core part of who I am and what I can offer to my clients. Because I understand human nature, I have a really good perception into what their prospects and clients are looking for and what they need. I don't work with formulas, but rather with deep and profound insight. What works for one company might not work with another company. I probe and ask the right questions, so I can develop a deeper understanding and guide my client in the right direction.

FAST RESULTS

In my experience working with small businesses, I have found that I have the ability turn the ship around really fast. If a company is in need, I can identify the problem and fix it – just as I did with Joey's autism, with my depression, and with our struggling business. I know how to help a company turn around by implementing systems for processes and for marketing. Once they get a new system in place, then they see success in a short amount of time.

RESOURCEFULNESS

I'm also very resourceful. For those business owners with substantial cash flow, we can implement some more advanced strategies or bring in outside resources. For a company with very little cash flow, I can work with what they have; because I've been there. Having a very tight marketing budget, I was able to help our tax preparation business book 800 tax appointments using just email marketing and a simple referral program. I know how to get by with whatever clients have at that particular moment and help move them to the next level of success.

EXPERIENCE AS A SMALL BUSINESS OWNER

Additionally, I have an advantage because I'm a business owner myself. Helping Joe with our tax and financial planning firms on a daily basis allows me to "play in the sandbox" and learn from practical experiences. I'm in a position to test marketing ideas or strategies before I recommend them to my clients. That allows me to make solid recommendations to my clients. Of course, some things fail and some things work, but I'm very careful about what I suggest. I can attribute this to the fact that I'm not a gambler. I don't like to put all my chips on the table. I've come to realize that I am only comfortable making sure bets. My clients appreciate my safe recommendations backed by my experience and personal results.

Chapter 17

Taking Care of Business

After competing to be the Ultimate Marketer of the Year and then becoming an Infusionsoft Certified Consultant just over a year ago, I hope to be a positive role model to others. I made it happen through my own resolve and faith, and I now realize the impact of simply taking action.

In addition to managing the marketing and operations of our family tax practice and our financial planning firms, I am now a full-time marketing and Infusionsoft consultant assisting my clients with a variety of services. Here are a few of the services I currently offer:

STRATEGIC MAPPING SESSIONS

For business owners that simply need a strategy for a new marketing campaign, I offer a Strategic Mapping Session. Prior to the 75-minute session, the client completes a Discovery Questionnaire to help us prepare for the call. During this interactive call, I assist the small business owner in building out a marketing campaign as a visual representation in Infusionsoft. I also give specific action items to the client for completing and launching that campaign. This is ideal for someone needing a jumpstart or wanting efficient strategies. I absolutely love starting with a clean slate, taking ideas, and collaborating with a small business owner to create a campaign "work of art."

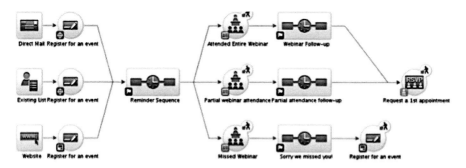

An example of a campaign Janette created using Infusionsoft's Campaign Builder for a company hosting a webinar.

PRIVATE COACHING PACKAGES

I also offer help with strategy, coaching, training, and/or implementation for a short-term project. My clients can purchase a Private Coaching Package giving them blocks of coaching and/or implementation hours to serve their specific needs. The first call is typically a Strategic Mapping Session, and all following hours are used to assist the client with completing and launching the new campaign.

VIP CONSULTING DAYS

For business owners that need to get away from the hustle and bustle of running their business, I offer a VIP Consulting Day. During this VIP Day in Phoenix, we put our noses to the grindstone for extreme focus and fast implementation. During the VIP experience, I assist my client with mapping out a marketing campaign in Infusionsoft. Then we spend the rest of the day building out the sequences and configuring the corresponding modules in Infusionsoft. It's amazing what we can accomplish in one day!

RETAINER MODEL

For companies that qualify, I offer a long-term commitment where I become a member of their team. By hiring me on retainer, it guarantees that I set monthly hours aside to work exclusively for that company. Monthly hours include strategy sessions, coaching, implementation, staff training, etc. to assist the small business with creating marketing campaigns and with maximizing their use of Infusionsoft. What I enjoy about this long-term commitment is becoming a member of their team and taking a huge stake in their success. I also get to know the company extensively and can contribute to their growth and achievements over time.

All of my current consulting and coaching services can be viewed on my website:

www.JanetteGleason.com

Chapter 18

The Best of Both Worlds

This newfound success has been wonderful for me because I can still be the mother and wife I've always wanted to be. I'm still here for my husband and my children as I work from home. I can get the children ready for school in the morning. I can pick them up from school at the end of the day, help them with their homework, and get dinner ready. I can do it all! I can have a career AND be a mom. It really is the best of both worlds for me.

I am so grateful that my husband Joe has supported me every step of the way. He is my biggest fan! It has taken some time for him and the kids to get used to having a working woman in the house. Some household chores have slipped on my part, and they have had to pick up the slack. We eat out a little more than we used to, but we enjoy visiting our favorite restaurants together. I appreciate my family's patience and understanding as we have had to restructure life somewhat in the Gleason household.

Here's the scoop about a typical day for me:

I wake up and start preparing for the day by packing the kids' lunches and backpacks and by laying out their clothes for school. Then I make breakfast, which is homemade pancakes, waffles, or French toast (I still haven't stopped spoiling them). Once the children are awake, I help them get ready and shuttle them off to school in our minivan. I walk them to their teachers each morning and spend a little time chitchatting with the other parents waiting with their children before the bell rings. After the principal delivers announcements, I give the kiddos hugs and kisses good-bye and head back to prepare for my workday.

My workdays vary, but I usually work from home in my home office (or at the kitchen table or by the swimming pool). Between coaching calls, I throw in loads of laundry or do some initial preparation for dinner. A few days out of the month I head out for the day to attend a training event, speak at a conference, facilitate an Infusionsoft User Group or meet up to work with one of my clients.

Typically, I am able to pick the kids up from school. Then it's time for the kids' snacks, play and rest. Then I take a few moments to wrap up my work for the day. The evening is set aside for our family dinners, homework, and quality time until the kids go to bed.

Don't get me wrong, my life isn't picture-perfect! Our kids sometimes argue with each other, resist their chores, and push me to the end of my rope. However, I absolutely love the flexibility of my schedule and being able to be around for my kids.

It's also important to me to set an example for our children, especially our girls. I want them to know that they too can have a balanced work and family life. Because I know my girls are watching and learning from me, I want to be the best role model I can be for them. As a parent, it's my job to encourage them to find their purpose and find the life/career that makes them completely happy. Joe and I support and encourage them and celebrate their individual gifts and talents.

Joey's progress has been amazing! His meltdowns are few and far between these days. He has outgrown many of his sensory issues, is making friends, and joyfully walks into his school every day. I am so proud of him, and I admire the smart, funny, and handsome boy that he is growing up to be. He still struggles with transitions and has some quirky behaviors. Each year as he matures, I am so grateful for how far he has come. The stability of me being home for him allows us to keep his routine the same, which makes for a happy boy.

Working from home has also allowed me to provide additional income for our family, and that makes me feel really satisfied. When I wasn't working, I felt guilty about spending money on myself. Joe never said anything to make me feel that way, and we have always been a team.

It was my own internal struggle and guilt that brought about those feelings. Joe and I still share all of our bank accounts and consider everything as "ours" - not yours and mine. It's my confidence and shift in mindset that allows me to indulge occasionally by going to an upscale salon or buying that cute new pair of boots I see at the store!

Best of all, I wake up each morning with excitement for what my day has in store for me. I am proud of my growing business, and I LOVE being a wife and mom.

Janette in a recent photograph with her ten-year old son, Joey (White Tank Regional Park, Arizona 2012)

Chapter 19

What's Next?

As a successful Mompreneur, I feel a deep sense of purpose now to help other moms experience the joy of working from home. My family has been blessed, and we are enjoying the fruits of our labor. Over the past several months, I've been searching for a way to give back and fulfill my desire for helping a large group of people. I believe my purpose is to support, nurture, empower, and uplift others, and I desire to continue helping in this way on a much larger scale.

With input from my husband, colleagues, mentors, and friends, I have started a program that will train and support mothers, wives, and spouses to become Virtual Assistants with an expertise in Infusionsoft.

This program is being created on a foundation with the following core values:

- We respect and support mothers who want to stay home with their children.
- We promote a balanced work and family life.
- We empower women to provide additional income for their households.

- We provide elite, exceptional, and efficient service.
- We help business owners perform their unique abilities.
- We conduct ourselves with class, initiative, and ambition.
- We support and uplift one another.

In order to serve as one of my Virtual Assistants, those who are interested will be required to submit an application and be accepted into the training program. Upon completion of my Virtual Assistant Training Program, each participant will need to pass a proficiency exam in order to begin working with clients. The Virtual Assistants will also participate in an ongoing coaching and training program.

This ongoing coaching and training will encompass four key areas:

1. **Infusionsoft Training:** During the Infusionsoft component of my coaching program, I will train on best practices in each module of the software. With feedback from the Virtual Assistants regarding the questions and needs that they have about the software, I will provide continued demonstrations of completing practical tasks in Infusionsoft.

2. **Business Operations:** My Virtual Assistants will be independent contractors and will become small business owners themselves! I will be teaching them how to effectively run a business from home and will cover topics such as accounting, scheduling, billing, etc.

3. **Lifecycle Marketing:** Because Infusionsoft has been built around the concept of Lifecycle Marketing, it will be important for the Virtual Assistants to have a thorough understanding of these marketing strategies. This will be important as they serve the needs of their clientele, but also for the growth and expansion of their own small businesses.

4. **Work/Family Balance:** I will bring in experts and guest speakers to give tips and suggestions for ways to live a balanced life. I will be building a community of families that can share ideas about topics ranging from recipes, family fun nights, and juggling chores to organizing your home, bonding with children, and creating family traditions.

This new endeavor is so exciting for me. The mothers I have begun to work with are also thrilled! I can hear the sparkle in their voices, and I share in the hope they have for this great opportunity.

Some moms in my program are working full-time outside of the home, and they simply desire to come home and raise their own children. They are tired and worn out. These moms wish they could be more involved at their children's school and have time to take them to after school activities and sports programs. I will guide these moms as they transition from their full-time job to working from home when the time is right.

Other moms now have school-aged children and are finding themselves looking to get back to work. With the economy as it is right now, it's hard for them to find a job, especially after being out of the workplace for an extended period of time. They are well-educated, intelligent woman trying to enter back into a career to no avail. For these moms that are willing and able to invest time in learning the software, they may soon have a new career ahead of them!

I also know moms that are currently stay-at-home mothers that wish to provide additional income for their families. Whether it's because they want to pay off credit cards, save for a down payment on a house, or go on a family vacation, they simply want to help out financially. These women are also looking for an opportunity to interact with other adults and/or begin a new career.

On the other hand, while consulting with my Infusionsoft clients, I see a real need for Virtual Assistance. I have found the following recurring themes in my discussions and interactions with many of them:

"I'm so busy running my business, and I would like someone to assist me on a part-time and as-needed basis."

"There is a learning curve for staying up-to-date regarding the most recent enhancements to the software, and I would like some support."

"I want my campaigns and emails customized for my particular business, but I need some help."

"I'm hesitant to go into the software and make changes because

I think I'm going to mess up or break something!"

"My current Virtual Assistant doesn't know enough about Infusionsoft."

Small business owners want someone dependable and efficient who keeps up-to-date with the changes and advancements in Infusionsoft. They would love to know they have someone they can trust to do quality work, work quickly yet accurately, and will follow through to complete the tasks assigned. This will allow the business owners to experience maximum benefits from the software, but still be able to focus on running their businesses.

An intelligent mother, wife, or spouse looking for flexible work paired with an Infusionsoft customer who needs reliable help – It's a perfect match!

As I venture out on this new business path, I so humbly reflect on some of the most painful times in my life, such as enduring our newborns with apnea, finding out Joey has autism, and dealing with anxiety and depression. I also with profound gratitude reflect on the amazing successes Joe and I have achieved in such a very short time. My greatest wish is to help other small business owners and mothers do the same.

Lessons Learned

With being a self-employed family for over fourteen years now and with operating four businesses, my husband and I have ridden the roller coaster of small business ownership. We've had abundantly successful times, but we've also had our share of struggles. The best thing that has come out of this wild ride has been the opportunity to learn some really valuable lessons.

DEVELOP SYSTEMS

I have learned that developing systems is the most important part of running a successful business. Those systems form the foundation upon which everything else runs. Once you have systems for your processes and procedures, you can plug anyone in and easily teach them the simple steps to follow. Systems also free up your time and allow you to be able to perform your unique abilities. If we had a system in place when our office manager quit in November of 2010, we could have plugged in a new employee more quickly. A big lesson was learned from that experience, and we've worked hard at putting our systems in place.

TAKE ACTION

You also have to take action, massive action, based on hard work with efficient time management. When I began working on customizing Infusionsoft for our business, I took action by researching, learning, and applying that knowledge. In only thirty days, I had created an entirely new marketing plan, and we were well on our way to doubling our tax preparation revenue. Please know that with taking action, you have to be willing to make changes. Just because something worked five years ago, it doesn't mean it's going to work today. We ran into this when our seminar marketing system stopped working, and we had no other methods in place. We realized it was time to make changes.

You should constantly be learning and implementing. Where there's no action, there's no progress. If you're not growing, you're dying. Currently, with a variety of marketing systems in place and with our multiple streams of income, Joe and I will never again be left without a chair when the music stops playing.

LIVE YOUR PURPOSE

An important piece of advice that comes from my own experience is to find your purpose and live it daily. For me, I know I thrive when I am nurturing, supporting, teaching, and uplifting others. Luckily for me, I am fulfilling these qualities not only in my professional life, but also as a mother and wife. If you can go about your day enjoying everything you do, you're living out your purpose - and to be able to find that is truly magical.

REFLECT

Finally, it's not just about where you're going. It's also about how far you've come. When I think about what's going to make me more successful, I'm always looking ahead to the next thing, but I also look back and reflect. I am amazed at how much I've grown and at how far I have come in a short amount of time. I was a stressed-out, depressed, stay-at-home mom. Now I'm a Mompreneur - a businesswoman with clients all over the world who also gets to run a loving household.

For me, the journey is just beginning, and I am really grateful for where I've been, blessed to be where I am now, and excited about where I'm going next!

Janette Gleason, an Infusionsoft Certified Consultant and Ultimate Marketer Finalist 2011, owns and manages a financial planning firm (Gleason Financial Group, LLC), a tax practice (Gleason Tax Advisory Group, LLC), an investment advisory firm (Gleason Investment Advisory, LLC), and a consulting firm (Gleason Consulting Group, LLC) along with her husband Joe. With a strong background in database marketing, she assists her companies and other small business owners with creating campaigns and systems that nurture prospects and help retain existing clients.

Janette grew up in the suburbs of Chicago and was educated at Augustana College in Rock Island, Illinois where she graduated Magna Cum Laude and earned her Bachelor of Arts degree in Elementary Education and Spanish.

After her ten-year teaching career, Janette became a stay-at-home mom to care for her family and support her autistic son. Now as a Mompreneur, Janette balances her work and family life so she can enjoy the best of both worlds.

Janette currently resides in Surprise, Arizona with her husband Joe, their three children, and their dog Buddy. When she isn't running one of their small businesses, consulting with clients, or being "mom," Janette enjoys reading, sewing, traveling, and spending time with friends and family.

Janette with her husband Joe and their 3 children: Jianna, Jillian, and Joey.

CPSIA information can be obtained at www.ICGtesting.com
Printed in the USA
LVOW10s1320120813

347483LV00006B/68/P